D0916985

LIFE IN THE TIME OF

MOCTEZUMA

and the Aztecs

Roy Burrell

Illustrations by Angus McBride

RSVP
RAINTREE
STECK-VAUGHN
P U B L I S H E R S
The Steck-Vaughn Company

Austin, Texas

Published by Raintree Steck-Vaughn Publishers, an imprint of Steck-Vaughn Company,

A Mirabel Book
Produced by Cynthia Parzych Publishing, Inc.
648 Broadway, N.Y., N.Y. l0012
Edited by: John Gilbert

Printed and bound in Belgium by Proost International Book Production

1 2 3 4 5 6 7 8 9 0 Pl 98 97 96 95 94 93

Library of Congress Cataloging-in-Publication Data

Burrell, Roy E.C. {Roy Eric Charles}
    Life in the time of Moctezuma and the Aztecs / written by Roy Burrell; illustrated by Angus McBride.
        p. cm. — (Life in the time of)
"A Mirabel book"—T.p. verso.
Includes index.
    Summary: Traces the history of the Aztec Indians, describing their religion, social structure, daily life, and the consequences of their contact with the Spanish during the reign of Moctezuma II.
        ISBN 0-8114-3351-X
        1. Aztec — Juvenile literature. {1. Aztecs.
2. Indians of Mexico.} I. McBride, Angus, ill.
II. Title. III. Title: Moctezuma and the Aztecs.
IV. Series.
F1219.73.B88 1993
972'.018—dc20
92-5823
CIP
    AC

COVER ILLUSTRATIONS:

Front: A young Aztec warrior in the uniform of a jaguar knight being inspected by his family. In the background is a temple in Tenochtitlán.

Back: Moctezuma is carried by bearers. In the foreground is a warrior with traditonal weapons, wearing a helmet adorned with eagle feathers.

PHOTO CREDITS:

Basilica of Guadalupe: 56
Bodleian Library, Oxford: 25, 26, 31, 32, 34
Bridgeman Art Library: 43
Chang, Heidi: 22, 41

8397 (93-94)

Contents

CHAPTER 1

Sacrifice

Map of the Aztec Empire at the time of the Spanish conquest in 1519.

In many parts of the world, there are legends that tell of the ritual killing of a person who had to die so that the tribe might live. Even the Bible speaks of human sacrifice. To Europeans of the sixteenth century, however, such tales were little more than fairy stories. They seemed to belong to a distant and almost unimaginable past.

Yet when the Spanish conquistadors began to press inland from the coasts of Mexico in the early 1500s, they discovered a civilization where human beings were being slain in thousands to appease the blood lust of the local gods. A force of Spanish invaders, commanded by the adventurer Hernán Cortés, were the first Europeans to make contact with a nationwide system of religious killings that played a central role in the life of the people known as the Aztecs.

The Aztecs believed that the gods they worshiped had created the universe by committing a kind of suicide. This universe would only continue to exist, so their priests told them, provided the gods were given an unending supply of sacrificed bodies, hearts, and blood.

CHOOSING THE VICTIM

Each year, one man was picked out to be the chief victim in the sacrificial ritual. The selection was made a year in advance so that full preparation for the event was assured. The young man was to impersonate the god *Tezcatlipoca,*

whom the Aztecs also called "Lord of the Night" and "Lord of the Smoking Mirror." The victim must therefore be of spotless reputation, so that a pure heart could be offered when the time arrived. For a year, the chosen one, dressed as the god in all his finery, could do more or less what he liked. He spent the days wandering around the capital city, Tenochtitlán (now Mexico City), amusing himself by playing on one of the several flutes that had been given to him. All the while he was treated by everyone as if he really were the god. One month before the ceremony, four young priestesses were married to him and saw to his every need and comfort.

The chosen victim willingly accepted his role in the solemn ritual. It may seem strange that he did not rebel or try to escape his fate. The reason is that religion played a much more important part in the life of the Aztecs than it does with us today. The merest word of a priest was something not to be questioned — only obeyed. In this case selection was a rare honor indeed.

Animals and birds were regularly sacrificed as well. Aztecs believed that the heart of any creature, even a humble fowl, was acceptable to the gods. Young boys were encouraged to bring a bird or small mammal to the temple, so that its heart could be torn out and offered to the Aztec deities. No difference was made for humans. The heart was cut out and burned, and the rest of the body disposed of in various ways.

HELL OR PARADISE

A second reason that the sacrificial victim agreed so readily to meet his fate was that he could expect special treatment in the world to come. The Aztecs were convinced that any person who died an ordinary death would go to a kind of underworld or hell, ruled over by the lord or lady of death. These were shadowy figures, usually drawn or carved wearing skull masks. However, a dead warrior or sacrificial victim went to what the Aztecs called *Ichan Tonatiuh*, or The Home of the Sun in the Sky. This was a glorious heavenly paradise which warriors slain in battle entered as a band of companions, traveling with the sun in its daily journey from east to west.

If the priests offered a youth the chance of entering this upper world, he could look forward to four years of bliss before being returned to life as a carefree butterfly. Who would not choose the certainty of an afterlife in heaven rather than the strong possibility of an eternity in hell?

THE CEREMONIAL CLIMAX

The sacrifice of the young man who was to impersonate the god formed a climax to the ceremony which often continued for several days, in the course of which enormous numbers of other victims were killed in a similar manner. Often, wars were fought solely for the motive of

Some sacrificial victims were offered the chance of avoiding death on the altar if they could successfully defend themselves against a joint attack by several armed warriors.

capturing live prisoners for this purpose. The Rededication of the Great Temple, for example, which was held at that point in the Aztec calendar when the "end of the century" arrived, required, by all accounts, thousands of human sacrifices. Endless lines of chosen men shuffled along the causeways that linked the island capital of Tenochtitlán with the mainland toward the immense square in the city center. There, in a five-day series of ceremonies, they were ritually slaughtered by the priests. Even the king took part in the killings. The sacrifice of the boy-god, however, was reserved for the fifth and final day.

As the youth, clad in the glorious colored robes of Tezcatlipoca, ascended the steep stone staircase that led to the shrine of the god, he dropped and broke his flutes one by one. At the top of the stairs he was seized by four priests who stripped him of his finery and stretched him across the *techcatl*, or stone altar. A fifth priest then slit his stomach and chest open with a sharp stone dagger and tore out his beating heart.

The priests kindled a new fire within a hole in the corpse. The heart was burned in a round stone brazier while another helper cut off the head. The body was rolled back down the stairs and the head placed in the *tzompantli*, or skull rack, which stood down in the square.

7

CHAPTER 2

Tenochtitlán

The Aztecs did not really know where they came from, nor who their ancestors had been. Sometimes they invented the history of their early days. Even so, certain facts from their distant past descended by word of mouth from generation to generation. Later, these stories were written down in a form of picture writing.

The name Aztec means "the people from Aztlán" and was probably given to them by their neighbors. Aztlán was the island in the middle of a lake which, according to Aztec legend, was their original home. They usually called themselves Mexica, and they spoke a language called Nahuatl, which was related to the languages of the Shoshone, Hopi, and Comanche. All these Indians, who lived in present-day northwest Mexico and southwest United States, led a wandering life, hunting, trapping, and occasionally fishing for food, probably around the middle of the twelfth century. At this time, Henry II was on the throne of England, soldiers from Europe were off on the Crusades, and no European dreamed of the existence of the Americas.

THE TOLTECS

For many centuries, the central valley of the Mexican mountains had been frequently overrun by various tribes, some of which were very complex cultures, with outstanding forms of art, architecture, and pottery. For some 200 years before the Aztecs arrived, the valley had been under the sway of the warlike Toltecs, who were famed as builders and craftsmen. The chief god of the Toltecs was Tezcatlipoca, Smoking Mirror; another was Quetzalcóatl, Feathered Serpent, both of whom would be adopted by the Aztecs.

The Toltec Empire was probably overthrown by the Culhuas. There followed many changes of allies and enemies, until, some time in the early 1300s, the Aztecs reached the shores of a large lake in the Valley of Mexico.

THE EAGLE ON THE CACTUS

According to the Aztlán legend, the Aztecs may have been driven from their first island home by unfriendly tribes who lived in the same area. They were spurred on by a promise made by their god Huitzilopochtli, Blue Hummingbird, that they should make their new home where

The Aztec god Tezcatlipoca.

they saw an eagle with a snake in its mouth, sitting on a cactus at the top of a hill. Their long trek ended at Lake Texcoco, at a height of over 7,000 feet (2,130 meters) above sea level, surrounded by active and dormant volcanoes.

The lake was a long, twisting stretch of marshy water, not very deep and divided into smaller swampy areas with names such as Zumpango, Xaltocán, Xochimilco, and Chalco. The islands on Texcoco and the adjoining lakes were ideal refuges and hiding places, safe from attacks by warlike neighbors. While penned up on one natural island, the men began to drain the marshy areas. They set up an altar and a small reed temple to Huitzilopochtli, built themselves simple huts, and thus laid the foundations of what was to become their chief town. They called it Tenochtitlán or "cactus rock."

The Aztecs had to work hard to make even a meager living from this new site and took anything that came easily to hand as food: fish, frogs, newts, insect eggs, cactus worms, and waterfowl. As time passed, the leaders of the tribe — ancestors of the future nobles — put up their houses near the temple; others had to take places farther from the center. Eventually, there was no more land left, and the poorer Aztecs were forced into desperate measures. They made new farms by dredging mud up from the bottom of the lake.

ABOVE: Aztecs with spears driving off an attack by a neighboring tribe.

BELOW: The eagle on the cactus, from Aztec legend.

FLOATING ISLANDS

After some years, the Aztecs became expert at island building. They started work on the *chinamitl* (floating island) or *chinampa,* as the Spaniards were later to call it, by collecting a drifting mass of small branches, grasses, and roots. When the raft of vegetation was big enough — varying in size from about 60 square yard (50 square meters) farms to much bigger farms with an average area of 2,000 square yards (1,675 square meters) — they drove straight poles in around the edges, tying them together with woven mats of reed. Then the builders carried earth and stones from the mainland and dumped them on top of the mat of branches until it sank to the bottom — never deeper than 10 feet (3 meters) below the surface and often shallower than that. The builders added more clay, stone, boulders, and gravel until the top could be seen less than a foot or so beneath the water level.

The next important step was to dig out the lake bottom between the new farm and its closest neighbors. The soft and extremely fertile mud was laid onto the new farm, making an island where none had previously existed. To prevent it being washed away, trees were planted around the boundaries so that the roots would bind the soil.

In places where the land was more like a swamp, with water no deeper than about 3 feet (1 meter), the Aztecs dug long trenches, or wider and deeper canals, through the mud. This drained the water into channels that could be controlled. The land left between the new ditches was then free of running water and just as fertile as any of the artificial islands.

From the earliest days, the Aztecs were compelled to pay tribute to their powerful neighbors on the mainland. This probably took the form of farm produce, as they gradually turned from hunting and gathering to growing crops on the handful of artificial islands surrounding the central natural island. The Aztecs grew mostly corn and beans with some amaranth, squashes, tomatoes, and chili peppers. Farmers who later moved to the mainland grew some

Aztec farmers building a "floating island" from compact masses of vegetation.

of these crops plus other plants that could not be raised on a chinampa. One such plant was the maguey cactus, from which the intoxicating liquor, *pulque,* was produced. They often terraced the hillsides and used local streams to provide water for their thirstier plants. But in the early days, the Aztecs had to trade with other tribes even for drinking water and depended on them, too, for timber and, later, building stone. All produce was brought in and out by dugout canoe.

At one stage, the Aztecs asked a nearby tribe for the hand of one of its beautiful princesses. The tribal leaders agreed, assuming she was to be married to a wealthy noble. But on the advice of the Aztec god, interpreted by his priests, the

princess was killed and flayed. When her father arrived to witness the wedding, he met a dancing priest clothed in her skin!

In the resulting battle, the Aztecs were confined to their island and had to drive off attacks with volleys of spears. The war continued for some time until the insult had been all but forgotten.

CAUSEWAYS

When conditions were more settled and the Aztecs had proved to their neighbors that they were strong enough to defend themselves, the nobles and the bravest warriors exchanged their reed huts for stone houses, and the tribal chiefs took on the power and authority of kings. As Tenochtitlán grew, contributions from the citizens went to pay workers to construct causeways to the mainland, so that people could walk to and fro.

A causeway was made by driving two parallel lines of strong wooden posts and then ramming loads of clay and dirt in between them until the surface was well above the water level. The Spanish soldiers who were eventually to conquer the city found that the causeways were wide enough for eight horsemen to ride side by side. One of the causeways was five miles long.

In time of war, to prevent attackers reaching the center of the city by causeway, the military commanders ordered gaps to be made at intervals in the paths. These gaps were normally bridged by wooden planks that could be taken away quickly if danger threatened. Farmers, too, used light wooden bridges to join their plot to that of a near neighbor. In this way people could go from chinampa to chinampa and finally reach a causeway.

Another major engineering feat was to bring in fresh drinking water from the streams that coursed down the higher slopes of the valley. This was achieved by building wooden aqueducts. The building and engineering skills of the Aztecs appear all the more remarkable when we realize that they never invented a practical wheel, which would have enabled them to make carts, nor domesticated any draft animals, which could have been used to haul heavy loads.

TOWNS AND KINGS

Gradually Tenochtitlán grew larger. In 1358 the city of Tlatelolco was founded, and fourteen years later a nobleman named Acamapichtli was recognized as king. Although the Aztecs still

Inhabitants of Tenochtitlán walking along one of the causeways that connected the city with the mainland.

paid tribute to the Tepanecs on the other side of the lake, serving them as soldiers, they prospered, gaining new farmland and trading connections with people in the tropical lowlands.

Acamapichtli died in 1391 and was succeeded by Huitzilihuitl II, who reigned for almost a quarter of a century. His brother, Itzcóatl, then ruled for fourteen years. During his reign, the Aztecs joined with other tribes to overthrow the Tepanecs and soon found themselves leaders of a new confederacy.

Moctezuma I, the son of Huitzilihuitl and his fourth wife, governed the island kingdom from 1440 to 1468. Moctezuma began the construction of aqueducts to bring fresh water to the city, built more artificial islands, and increased the area of the capital. As he extended his conquests, he demanded tribute from distant towns and villages. The Aztecs were thus introduced to exotic goods, such as cotton for clothing, tropical bird feathers for decoration, cocoa, and gold dust. By the time Moctezuma I's grandson, Axayacatl, came to the throne, the empire stretched as far as the Pacific coast. In 1502, his son, Moctezuma II, the last of the powerful Aztec kings, began his reign.

RUNNING THE CITY

As Tenochtitlán grew in size, providing homes for an ever increasing population, methods had to be found to govern the city and provide for general needs. Officials had to be appointed to make sure the people had enough food and water, to dispose of refuse and establish standards of hygiene, to keep law and order, to maintain the temples, to arrange the religious ceremonies, and to regulate all aspects of everyday life.

To make administration easier, the city was divided into a number of smaller areas. Those who lived in a particular area were, in many instances, related to one another, forming a clan. Every clan area possessed its own temple, which was usually situated in an open square. The Aztec name for this living area was *calpulli*. Each calpulli was expected to provide groups of people to work on public projects such as building dams, canals, sewers, and so on.

There was a kind of local council of elders, whose senior representatives traveled to the city center every day to receive their latest instructions. They were told what tasks had to be done by their own workers and the number of young men or older, more experienced adults required for army service. The councillors also ran the calpulli's law courts, which were authorized to deal with petty crime. More serious cases were passed on to the king's courts.

The council had the responsibility of collecting tribute taxes from their local citizens. It also parceled out farmland to those young men who were thought to be old enough to get married.

The smaller clan areas were grouped together into larger administrative regions. These, in their turn, had their own temples and marketplaces where goods produced in that region were exchanged for tribute from defeated or subject tribes. This tribute was largely in the form of food. During the later years of Aztec history, there were so many people living in Tenochtitlán and the other large cities that the local farmers could not possibly grow all the food that was needed. So, to make up for the shortfall, the Aztecs were compelled to keep up pressure on their neighbors, sometimes going to war with them for the flimsiest reasons, in order to ensure that tribute foodstuffs continued to flow in.

Estimates vary as to the likely extent of

The funeral of a peasant with the body of the dead person wrapped and tied in the crouched position, according to custom.

Tenochtitlán at the height of its power. The invading Spaniards were certainly astonished at its size and splendor. They had never in their lives seen so vast a city. There is no evidence that the Aztecs ever ran a census to count the number of inhabitants; but considering how closely the buildings were packed together near the center of the city, it is likely that about a quarter of a million people lived in the capital at that time.

BURIAL CUSTOMS

There were no cemeteries in Tenochtitlán. The body of a dead person was normally tied up in a crouched position with strips of cloth. Then, while the proper prayers were chanted, the body was sprinkled with water and offered gifts of incense, clothing, and colored thread. A precious or semiprecious stone was placed in the corpse's mouth. For poor people, this token was usually a chip of obsidian.

The Aztecs believed that it took a common person four years to reach the lowest level of the underworld and that he or she needed to take a small dog as a guide. The dead dog and the body were therefore burned together and their ashes buried under the earth floor of the hut. Of course, if the deceased person was rich, of noble birth, or of warrior status, the remains were buried separately with great honor and ceremony.

THE CITY CENTER

Visitors to Tenochtitlán could not fail to be impressed by its fine buildings. Farmers, for example, might bring in their families from the surrounding countryside either to trade produce or just to take part in a religious service or sacrificial rite.

Disembarking from their dugout canoe, they would walk along one of the causeways, hastily passing by the public lavatory boats moored alongside. These were cleared regularly and their contents used as fertilizer on the chinampas.

Leaving behind the open land of the farms, they soon came to the living and working quarters of the city craftsmen. Nor could they help comparing their own simple huts with the larger, more comfortable houses of those who made pottery, wove baskets, cast silver and gold for

The temple district at the center of Tenochtitlán.

jewelry, or followed one of the many other trades that helped to keep the city busy and thriving. And the contrast was greater still as they strolled the streets lined with the well constructed stone houses of the nobles. Most had two stories and white painted walls, with their own flower beds, ornamental pools, and even fruit orchards.

The rich residential district gave way to the area occupied by the huge buildings of government, religion, and royalty. Many of these impressive official buildings had their walls painted in very bright colors — red, blue, green, and white.

The climax of the family trip was their arrival in the immense central square with its 200-foot (60-meter-high) pyramids, surmounted by altars to the gods. This central walled area, measuring more than 500 yards (450 meters) on each of the four sides, enclosed at least fifty buildings for religious purposes of various types. The farmer and his family surely must have been dazzled by all this magnificence.

CHAPTER 3

Moctezuma and His Nobles

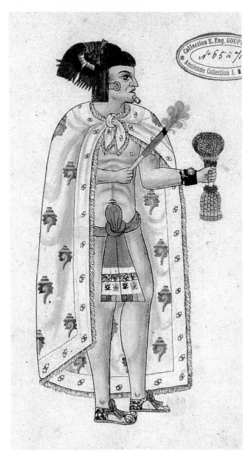

An Aztec nobleman wearing typically fine and elegant clothing.

When Moctezuma II began his reign, the Aztec Empire had reached its greatest extent, and his capital of Tenochtitlán was as large as it was ever to be under Aztec rule. Indeed, it was almost certainly bigger, with more people living there than any other city in America — or, for that matter, even in Europe.

As the years passed, the Aztec kings had grown more and more remote from their people. They rarely appeared in public. Inside the royal palace, very few of their subjects were even permitted to look directly at their ruler. When the king delivered a judgment or gave an order, he would normally whisper the proper words into the ear of a court official who then repeated the pronouncement aloud.

Because the Aztec lands had swollen so enormously, they were no longer easy to govern. It was impossible for the king to control the whole empire entirely by himself.

THE KING'S HELPERS

To assist the king there was a council of nobles and elders who gave advice whenever it was required. This council also chose the person to be the next king when the present one died.

To be a noble, one had to be fortunate enough to be the child of a noble father. The only other way into the exclusive and privileged circle was to earn a reputation for bravery in battle. Although in theory this route was open to the common people, few of them were ever able to make use of it. In fact, Moctezuma's father had insisted that no one could call himself noble unless he could trace his ancestry back to Acamapichtli, the very first king. Proving this was very complicated and difficult because of the "harem" system of marriage that existed. Members of the ruling class, from the king downward, were not only permitted but expected to have many wives.

When Moctezuma went to war, won victories, or demanded tribute, a huge army of clerks and officials went, too. They had to make sure that the cotton, feathers, gold, and cocoa sent by the defeated tribes were sufficient in quantity and quality and that they arrived on time.

The chief assistant to the king was known as the "Snake Woman." Oddly enough, the person holding this office was always a man.

RULES AND REGULATIONS

Moctezuma had inherited from earlier kings a complicated list of rules and rituals for himself, his courtiers, nobles, and warriors, and for

all of his subjects in the vast Aztec Empire.

When the king made one of his rare journeys about the city, he was carried on a kind of litter, which was brightly painted and decorated. Moctezuma wore an enormous headdress of green quetzal bird feathers and precious stones. His bearers wore very colorful and patterned clothing. Their cloaks and capes were adorned and embroidered but not so dazzlingly as those of the king.

Inside the palace, anyone who wished to come into the king's presence, even warriors and nobles, had to do so barefoot and in shabby old cloaks. But clothing rules applied outside the palace as well. There were regulations concerning style of footwear and laws that controlled the design, size, and positioning of gold body jewelry. Nor was any noble permitted to wear a mantle that came down past the knees. If he did, he might be killed, unless he could prove that he wanted to cover up ugly battle scars.

Such rules meant little to ordinary folk, who were quite unable to afford expensive shoes and jewels. Yet they were forbidden, on pain of death, to wear any garment of cotton but had to make do with clothes woven from cactus or palm tree fiber. If, by some unlikely chance, a commoner were to visit the palace, he had to make sure he was not breaking any of these laws.

The entrance to the royal palace in Tenochtitlán, the outside of which was painted in brilliant colors.

Once inside, he would be shown to a room on his own: no worker was allowed to occupy the same room as a noble, let alone the king.

Only nobles were permitted to build themselves two-story stone houses. The cream of the nobility controlled the use of land and the farmers who worked it.

Yet for all their privileges, the nobles were, in some ways, subject to harsher laws than farmers and workmen. For example, the law said that the extremely potent pulque could only be drunk by people over the age of fifty. This regulation was usually flouted but if, by bad luck, a noble was found to be intoxicated, he could be executed on the spot.

A similar punishment awaited any noble who ran off with another man's wife. People further down the social scale ran no risk of this. They could not afford, nor were they allowed, more than one spouse at a time.

THE PALACE

We do not know for certain what Moctezuma's palace was like. The site was later built over and is now occupied by the National Palace, offi-

An Aztec king being carried around Tenochtitlán by bearers.

the main square of the pyramid temples in the center of Tenochtitlán. The Aztec word for it was *tecpan*, and it was extensive enough to cover an area greater than three full-sized football fields.

The site included not only the royal residence but also the main government offices such as the central law courts, where prisoners were both tried and kept in captivity. In addition, there were storerooms for the huge piles of tribute, plus living and working quarters for armies of civil servants and skilled craftsmen, some of whom produced the splendid feathered headdresses, cloaks, and gold ornaments worn by the nobles and the king himself.

To avoid having to hunt or trap the exotic birds that provided the bright feathers so highly valued by the Aztecs, quetzals and parrots were kept on the grounds. They were fed, looked after, and plucked by special workers to produce a constant supply of brilliant red and green feathers.

There were squares, courtyards, orchards, pools, and even a royal zoo. Here jaguars, foxes,

cial residence of the Mexican president. However, the remarks of some Spaniards who actually visited Moctezuma give an idea of the palace's size and splendor.

It stood just outside and to the southeast of

snakes, and other wild beasts from the tropics were fed on birds, dogs, and even the headless bodies of human sacrifices.

DINING WITH MOCTEZUMA

There were so many rooms in the palace, said the Spanish visitors, that people often got completely lost. The main dining room had a wooden throne of state. In front of the throne was a low wooden table, covered with finely woven cloths. There was much activity for serving women came and went constantly, bearing freshly cooked foods, and taking away the dirty dishes.

Meals might include the round, flat corn cakes that are known in modern Mexico as tortillas, corn with minced or diced meat and doused in peppery sauces (tamales), beans, turkey, quail, fish of all kinds, lobsters, rabbits, small dogs, rats, deer, and a multitude of other dishes. The palace cooks boasted that they had over 2,000 recipes that they could serve to order. For dessert, the guests enjoyed a wide range of local and tropical fruits. All through the meal, troupes of performers kept the diners entertained. Among their number were dancers, singers, dwarfs, acrobats, jugglers, and jesters.

When the last scraps of meat had been finished off and the last cups of chocolate and vanilla drunk, the nobles respectfully took their leave of their royal master and threaded their way homeward. On their way out they would have admired the red, green, blue, and white colors in which many of the inside and outside walls were painted. They would have passed by statues of animals and gods and relief carvings of the same subjects on the walls. Everywhere were vast beds of sweetly scented flowers.

Moctezuma neglected no opportunity to show his nobles and anyone else — either friend or possible foe — what a mighty ruler he was and what a large and powerful empire he controlled.

King Moctezuma entertaining his guests at dinner.
The meal comprised a rich assortment of meats, poultry,
fish, and desserts, accompanied by dancers, singers,
and jugglers.

CHAPTER 4

Gods, Temples, and Priests

The temple of *Huitzil-opochtli* stood on top of a lofty pyramid in the main square of Teno-chtitlán. He was the most important of all the Aztec gods. Tezcat-lipoca, too, was greatly venerated, particularly among the inhabitants of Texcoco, a city on the mainland east of Teno-chtitlán. He also had a temple in the capital.

Quetzalcóatl was a god whom the Aztecs had taken over from the Toltecs, the previous rulers of the valley. The Toltecs had themselves "borrowed" him from previous civilizations. He was worshiped as the god of learning, priesthood, and the winds. His name and reputation were to play a significant part in the final overthrow of the empire.

Tláloc, the god of rainfall, was respected because he decided whether the farmers' crops would grow or not. He, too, had an important place in the lists of the gods and a temple all to himself in Tenochtitlán's main square.

Every Aztec settlement of any size possessed a temple or shrine dedicated to at least one god. Many of these deities were worshiped in various places, under different names, and with multiple roles. There were certainly more than a hundred of them. These heavenly beings had charge of the sun, the moon and the earth, fire and water, mountains and volcanoes, birth and death, cacti and flowers, love and beauty, feasting and dancing,

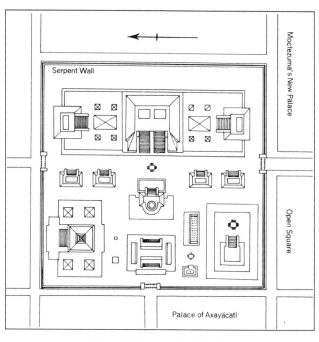

Plan of the temple district in the center of Tenochtitlán.

merchants and crafts-men, warfare and hunt-ing, games, numbers, and many more aspects of everyday life. Some deities were in control of opposites — there was a god of night and day, right and wrong, a god of life and death, and a god of good and evil.

THE TEMPLE DISTRICT

The Aztecs believed that the more important a deity, the nearer to heaven his shrine should be. So they kept on building new temples on top of old ones, increasing their height by using huge blocks of stone, hauled in on rollers from the sur-rounding mountains. The Aztecs knew nothing of carts and did not use wheels. They had no draft animals. Roads were well-worn paths, and everything, even the heaviest loads, had to be transported by human effort. The blocks were maneuvered into position, then carved and shaped by an army of sculptors and masons, using cop-per chisels and hard, round stones.

The important temples of Tenochtitlán honored the gods Huitzilopochtli, Quetzalcóatl, Tezcatlipoca, Tláloc, and several others. They stood in the very center of the city, in a vast enclo-sure that measured about 550 yards (500 meters) along each of its four sides. The area was marked off by a stone wall of sculptured serpents.

At ground level was the skull rack where the

heads of the human sacrifices were stored. Nearby were the *calmécac*, or priests' school, and the ball court. The calmécac was attended by the children of the nobles. They were taught by priests, and many of these children became priests themselves when they grew up.

The game played on the ball court seems to have been a kind of basketball. The players used only their knees and hips to shoot a hard rubber ball through a stone hoop that stuck out sideways from the surrounding wall. The religious meaning of the game remains unclear.

The temple pyramid of the god Huitzilopochtli.

PICTURE WRITING

Young trainee priests were taught to read and write. Instead of using letters and sentences, they wrote in pictures that showed different meanings. To indicate someone speaking, they drew a blue speech "bubble" coming from a person's mouth. A line of small black, bare footprints meant walking or going on a longer journey.

To express an abstract idea, the writer would think up two or three other words and draw and combine them into a sort of pun. If English worked the same way, we might draw a cat and a log for the word "catalog." The reader had to decide whether the picture symbols (glyphs) meant "catalog" or literally "cat" and "log." In the same way, we might write a picture sentence that the reader would recognize as "eye, can, tree, sister, lemon, drink," and perhaps work out that what is meant is "I can't resist a lemon drink." This seems a hard way to get across a sentence with a precise meaning, but an educated Aztec would have had no trouble with it.

Paper was called *amatl* and was made from the inner bark of certain trees, peeled from the trunk, steeped in water, and then hammered into long sheets. It was cut into rectangles or folded into maplike creases and treated so that it could be used for clear line drawings in colored inks.

A young man was permitted to leave the school when he was twenty. He could, if he wished, get married and would therefore need a profession. He could work as a civil servant, checking taxes and tribute, treat the sick with herbal potions and prayers, become a full-time priest in a temple, or set up as an astrologer to predict the future.

THE AZTEC CALENDAR

The diagram shown on the next page illustrates the one used by the Aztec priests to keep a record of the passing of the seasons. They knew that there were roughly 365 days from one midsummer to the next. But they also regulated their activities by a holy calendar, supposedly given to human beings by Quetzalcóatl.

The small disc representing the *tonalpohualli*, or holy calendar, is marked with thirteen lugs, numbered in sequence and fitted into slots on the day-names wheel. There were twenty numbers on the bigger wheel. The year started on alligator 1, followed by wind 2, house 3, lizard 4, and so on. The "week" ended when the little wheel had turned for thirteen separate days. Then the next week began ocelot 1, eagle 2, and so on. Two hundred and sixty days later, the cycle was complete, and both wheels would now read "alligator 1." Although there were several

*ABOVE: Aztec laborers using rollers to move
the stones for building a temple.
BELOW: The Aztec calendars.
The normal everyday calendar is on the right,
the religious one on the left.*

of our months still to go to complete an annual cycle, the Aztec holy calendar then began again. The two calendars were now out of step with each other, and it would be fifty-two years before they came together again.

THE END OF THE CENTURY

The Aztecs believed that the day when this happened would bring all kinds of bad luck. On this day the sacred temple flame was allowed to go out, statues of the family and local gods were deliberately broken, and men threw away or smashed all their other possessions. Women and children were locked up to prevent them being changed into animals. Devils were expected to devour the entire world and bring endless night.

Priests stripped the bark off a slender tree branch at the end of each natural year. When they had fifty-two in their bundle, they knew the terrible "end of the century" had arrived and that it was time for the ceremonies. They painted their bodies with black dye made from crushed beetles, sang and danced for hours on end, and prepared for their human sacrifice as the climax to the final five days of the century. This was also the time for the king and priests to enlarge the temple by building over and around it. Only when these rituals were complete could normal life begin anew.

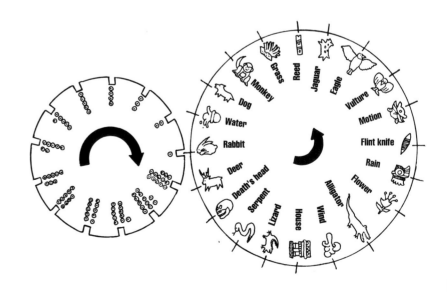

CHAPTER 5

Battle and Tribute

Every Aztec boy had to do military service, and some went on to become members of a standing army. A soldier's functions would include guarding the king's palace, but he would be likely to have many experiences of active service. Raw recruits, part-time soldiers, and professional warriors had their own form of dress and decoration to show where they stood in the military social scale.

Because the authorities required so many human sacrifices for their gods, the prime object in battle was not to kill the enemy but to capture him alive. This strategy was finally to lead to the Aztecs' overthrow by the Spaniards.

The main Aztec army consisted of amateurs and professionals, with their own commanders, often under the supreme command of the king. It was supported by auxiliaries such as messengers, surgeons, and engineers. But despite its fearsome reputation, it seldom attacked in mass formation. And once the battle had begun, the whole engagement tended to become a seething mass of individual combats.

CAPTURING PRISONERS

Every young man was expected to take at least one prisoner. Even the son of a noble was not allowed to wear traditional finery but just a rough cape of cactus fiber, until he brought in his first captive. Then, too, when a boy was on the verge of manhood, his hair was cut, leaving a long tress hanging down the back of his neck. This would not be removed until he took his first prisoner. After that glorious achievement, he was permitted to grow his hair over the right ear.

A really daring soldier might advance into battle naked, armed simply with a throwing net. With this he would hope to entangle his enemy and take him alive. On the other hand, the warrior who never captured anyone was mocked, not only by his comrades but by people at home when the war was over, and he returned from battle.

Once a young soldier had taken four captives he became a *tequiua*. He could then expect a

Prisoners of war. Taking a prisoner was one of the highest aims of the young warrior.

share of any tribute and was permitted to wear a much more ornate cape and decorations. Moreover, he could now participate in discussions about the conduct of the war and might be called upon to perform high military or civilian duties as a commander, official, or judge.

The bravest warriors who took the most captives could look forward to royal favors, advancement, or even promotion to the nobility, earning them the right to build a two-story house and be given more farmland. But some, in spite of their heroism, were not considered worthy of high office, perhaps because they were too violent and unpredictable. Instead these would then be entitled to wear a jaguar skin or a wooden helmet adorned with eagle feathers and were almost worshiped as the sun god's chosen men.

ARMS AND ARMOR

Although the Aztecs sometimes used the bow and arrow, they preferred the spear. This was normally hurled from an *atlatl,* or spear-thrower. The other principal weapon was a wooden club set with razor-sharp slivers of obsidian. Some soldiers were equipped with slings for throwing stones, but these were not thought to be very effective. Many carried around wooden or wickerwork shields covered with hide or feathers. Sometimes these shields would be decorated with brilliantly painted shapes and symbols.

Most warriors wore armor of quilted cotton, soaked in saltwater to stiffen and strengthen it. As Cortés and his soldiers were later to discover, this type of protection was almost as effective as steel and a good deal cooler to fight in.

FILLING THE SKULL RACKS

In times of peace, when there was a shortage in the supply of captives, the Aztecs had two methods of making sure of enough sacrificial victims. They either arranged what were known as "wars of flowers," or they deliberately engineered wars with other tribes.

The first type of battle was an army exercise in which priests acted as referees. When it appeared that sufficient men had been taken captive, they stopped the fighting. But sometimes the combatants became so heated and enraged that a full-scale war developed, and the priests were powerless to halt it.

The other way of keeping the skull racks full was for the Aztecs to pick a quarrel with a particular tribe, claiming they had been insulted. They might demand tribute or complain that existing tribute was too late, too small, or of poor quality.

One favorite excuse for war was that the outsiders had attacked or robbed Aztec merchants.

Aztec warriors in battle using typical armor and weapons.

A part of Moctezuma's tribute roll, illustrating some of the goods that conquered tribes were required to offer the Aztecs.

Such merchants, in the course of their normal business of exchanging goods with other cities, were also expected to do a little spying on the side. Once they had obtained information about the other side's strength and will to resist, an Aztec delegation from Tenochtitlán would perhaps demand tribute, favorable terms of trade, and the building of a temple to Huitzilopochtli in the enemy's city, at their own expense. Then, at intervals of about three weeks, other delegations would arrive from Texcoco and Tlacopan, with more demands and threats. They would leave gifts of spears and shields so that their victims could not say they had no chance when the fighting started.

PAYING TRIBUTE

Victory in war brought in prisoners and tribute. And even though the Aztecs were sometimes beaten in battle, they received vast amounts of tribute from defeated and subjected tribes. The goods that flowed into their storehouses included cotton fiber, wood for building and for fuel, stone for houses and temples, seashells for decoration and use as musical instruments, jewelry, precious stones, gold dust, silver, copper, furs, jaguar skins, headdresses and exotic feathers, shields, pottery, paper, tobacco, and foodstuffs. In addition to everyday items, like corn and corn flour, chilies, fruits, prickly pears, and tomatoes, there were more valued imported items, such as cocoa, chocolate, vanilla, and even pineapples.

At the time of the Spanish conquest, nearly 400 towns and cities were paying tribute to the Aztecs. The Aztec Empire had reached its peak.

25

CHAPTER 6

Women and Girls

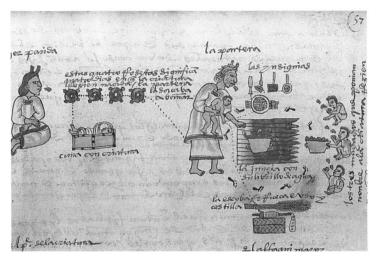

The Aztec birth ceremony. The midwife is shown bathing the newborn baby girl while the three seated boys are ready to call out the name she has already chosen.

All Aztec children were brought up to believe that the world was a place of hardship and suffering. And as in so many cultures, past and present, the roles of both sexes were determined at an early age. A boy had many opportunities. He could hope to rise in the social scale, he enjoyed a more complete education, he would experience the excitements and dangers of army life, and he would have access to a variety of crafts and professions. A girl, on the other hand, was expected to stay at home and to work for her parents and later for her husband and children. The nature of her future life was defined almost at birth when she was presented with a needlework box, spindles and shuttles for weaving, and a tiny toy broom.

THE NAMING DAY

The arrival of a baby girl was celebrated with a party, with plenty of food and drink. If the birth had occurred on an unlucky day, the party was postponed for a while until the fortune-teller could choose a more auspicious day. The Aztecs were very superstitious and always called in an astrologer before doing anything important. The astrologer would select the best day to begin building a house or to make a business deal, even, in the case of the king, to declare war.

Once the lucky day was chosen, the midwife who had helped at the delivery swaddled the infant in a blanket or sheet and gently laid her on the floor. She then placed the customary gifts one by one in the baby's hand and told her how to use them. The relatives made speeches in which they stressed the little girl's role in life: back-breaking work, with very little reward. It was usual to invite three or four little boys to the party. They watched and waited anxiously and, when the midwife finally announced the name of the new arrival, the boys rushed off in excitement to shout the name aloud to the neighbors.

HOUSEHOLD TASKS

Girls born into an ordinary working family learned at a very early age to help with simple domestic jobs such as cooking and cleaning. From the age of about five, they swept the dirt floor of the hut, gathered berries, and collected branches and sticks for the fire. When they were a little older, they learned how to spin cotton or maguey thread on a hand-held spindle. At this age they also helped to look after the younger children of the family. They soon knew how to deal with babies, and this prepared them for the time when they would have their own children to care for.

In due course the child was taught to weave

Aztec girls carrying out household tasks such as weaving and dyeing thread.

by watching her mother at work on the typical Aztec loom. This consisted of a couple of battens about 3 feet (1 meter) long, around which went the warp threads — maguey fiber for poor families, cotton for rich ones. The weaver leaned back into a waist belt attached to each end of the batten in order to keep the warps taut and tightly stretched, and then darned the weft thread through them. Colors were obtained by first dipping the threads in dyes made from the leaves, stems, roots, and berries of many different plants.

EDUCATION

Together with boys, girls were constantly exhorted to lead an upright and god-fearing life. But in contrast to their brothers, they were not taught how to read or write, nor trained for a profession or trade. Yet even those from a poor background received the rudiments of education between the ages of twelve and fifteen at a *cuicacalli* or house of song. Here they were taught a simplified version of the hymns and chants that were so much a part of Aztec reli-

gious life. Like the boys, they would be punished for misbehaving. They might be beaten or pricked with cactus thorns, or even held over burning chilies and made to inhale the pungent, choking smoke.

Daughters of the nobles naturally had a much easier life. For them the daily round was not nearly so arduous. Surrounded by comfort, they were sent to a kind of nunnery school taught by ex-priestesses who had grown too old to continue serving in the temples. Here they learned how to weave, sew, and embroider, how to behave, and how to recite the songs and prayers that were used at religious services and sacrifices.

One invaluable thing a girl might expect to learn from her mother was to use herbal remedies. The mother was the family doctor. She would send for a professional only if the illness were more serious than she could cope with. After her children were grown up, if a woman was particularly interested and skilled, she might herself become a professional, doctoring the families of her neighbors with the proper chants and prayers, and getting them to take vegetable medicines made from turnips, juniper berries, cacti of various species, or some of the thousand or so other medicinal herbs known to the Native Americans in those days.

27

Large crowds attended the markets where foodstuffs, cloth, pottery, and luxury goods were normally exchanged by barter.

THE MARKETPLACE

Women were also expected to do the shopping, and some stayed to sell as well as to buy. A market was held every few days in the center of the city. These markets were well attended, with thousands of people milling around, and doubtless they were very colorful and noisy. But because the Aztecs had no metal coins, the usual system of trading was barter. Customers had to try to exchange what they brought for what they wanted.

People would perhaps offer a length of cloth to swap for a couple of clay pots. Men from the surrounding hill districts often arrived with goose feathers, the hollow quills of which were packed with gold dust. If the two items involved in the bargaining were not exactly equal in value, the difference could be made up with varying numbers of cocoa beans, which were used as small change.

The wives or daughters of farmers brought in whatever they had to spare — farm produce, handmade pottery, baskets, or cloth — and spread it out on woven mats on the ground. Then they sat behind their piles of goods and waited for customers. Sellers of more valuable things could afford to set up wooden stalls. Each seller had to pay a fee for the use of her space. This was collected by an official who wandered through the market checking weights and measures and trying to make sure that goods were up to standard. A woman or girl who sold rot-

ten fruit, for example, could have all of her stock confiscated. Anyone discovered stealing was tried immediately by the market court. If found guilty, he or she could be clubbed to death on the spot.

The goods on sale in the market were many and various. There were pots, stone axes, copper needles, obsidian mirrors, paint, cloth, leather, sandals, furs, parrot feathers, and tobacco. Foodstuffs ranged from salt, fish, and turkeys to hot tortillas and honey cakes. And for those who could afford them, there was everything from gemstones and jewelry to canoes and slaves.

MARRIAGE

An older wife could also become a midwife or a marriage broker. A man's family would usu-ally send for the marriage broker as soon as the prospective husband was about twenty years old. A girl was ready to be married when she was aged sixteen. The broker was sent to the girl's family where the offer of marriage was normally refused two or three times before being accepted.

Sometimes young people chose their own partners, but arranged marriages were far more common. It was legal for rich men to have several wives but, apart from royalty and the higher nobility, one wife at a time was the rule among most of the people. As usual, an astrologer chose a lucky day for the marriage ceremony.

Before the wedding, the bridesmaids bathed the bride-to-be and decorated her legs with red feathers and her face with yellow paint. The girl's mother and future mother-in-law gave gifts of cloth

In the marriage ceremony the cloaks of the bride and groom were tied together symbolically.

and clothing. On the wedding day, the matchmaker or broker washed out the bride's mouth and then fed both partners with four mouthfuls of sauce and tamales — very hot crushed corn and meat.

Women busy preparing a meal.

The marriage broker led the girl to the groom's house and married them by tying together the corners of their cloaks. The happy couple were then shut up alone for four days while the feasting went on. This feast was attended by relatives and, if the family could afford it, many rare and expensive foods were served. Guests drank intoxicating pulque, and the men smoked tobacco in cane pipes.

When a young bride became pregnant, the fact was announced by the young woman's parents to important noble families in the neighborhood and to all the young woman's near and distant relatives. Then came another feast, during which the couple were reminded of their duties to their ancestors and to the gods.

Just before the expected date of birth, the senior relatives met in the young woman's parents' home to decide on a midwife. When her time came, she was taken to a special room for the birth. In a wealthy family, this might be the saunalike bathhouse. Then the baby was born. If the new arrival was a girl, she could expect a life much like that of her mother.

CHAPTER 7

Clothes and Beauty

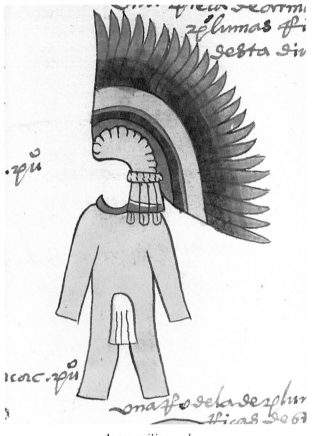

Aztec military dress.

Although Tenochtitlán lay at more than 7,000 feet (2,130 meters) above sea level, the weather was mild throughout most of the year. As a result, Aztecs, in common with many other Native Americans, had no need to wear much heavy clothing. We possess few of their actual garments, since clothing materials do not normally survive through the centuries except in lands with exceptionally dry climates. So we have to rely on statues, pictures, or written descriptions to get any notion of what their dress looked like. Fortunately, the Aztec system of writing contained a large number of human figures, so it has become possible for us to get a rough idea of what they wore.

THE MAXTLATL

Men and boys needed little more than a loincloth, known as a *maxtlatl*. This garment was worn by everyone — rich or poor, powerful or unimportant. The only variations were the materials from which it was made and the designs which appeared on it. For the well-to-do, cotton was the standard material; the poor had to make do with fiber from cactuses or palm trees. The cloth was woven in a long strip on a small loom. The finished maxtlatl was taken between the legs and around the waist. The end was then tucked in to make all secure.

Whether the maxtlatl was of maguey fiber or pure cotton, completely plain or highly decorated, as it was for officials, priests, nobles, or army commanders, it always had to be tucked in simply because the Aztecs had no buttons. So all forms of garment had to be fastened either by being tucked in or tied — hence the custom of joining the cloaks of a newly married couple by knotting them together.

Slaves, too, wore the maxtlatl, but those being sold in the marketplace were also forced to wear a wooden collar around their neck. A farmer would wear nothing more than a maxtlatl, and even when working on his farm with digging stick or hoe, his feet were bare.

It seems from Aztec pictures that children were allowed to go around completely naked — at least when they were very young and then only in their own homes. Boys wore a belt at the waist with a scrap of cloth dangling from it at the front. When they grew up, they might carry this fashion into the army. Military dress

31

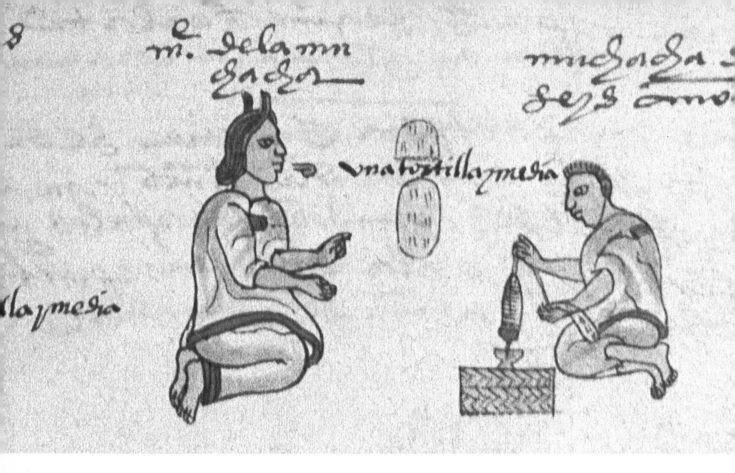

A woman teaching her daughter to spin.

styles often comprised a sort of body stocking, still with the scrap of cloth in place, even though the body was entirely covered.

WOMEN'S CLOTHES

Girls and women also had a basic dress style, which consisted of a length of cloth about 6-10 feet (2-3 meters) long and 3 feet (1 meter) wide. This was wrapped around the waist and fell to the ankles. It, too, was secured by pushing in the free end behind the thickness of cloth already in position, rather as we today wrap a towel around ourselves after a bath.

The simplest form of upper garment was a somewhat shorter length of maguey or cotton fiber, folded over and sewn at the two lower sides. This left room for the arms. There was a circular hole cut for the head. More elaborate versions of this garment had a properly tailored neckline and short sleeves. The housewife would do any sewing that was necessary with more maguey fiber or cotton, threaded through a copper needle or a spine from a cactus plant.

As already mentioned, coloring was achieved by dyeing the thread in various solutions of vegetable extracts or by steeping it in a liquid made from dead insect bodies. Cochineal insects, for example, gave a red tint. Incidentally, these same cactus insects are still used today in America and Britain to produce a type of food coloring.

CLOTHING LAWS

An Aztec man would often wear a cloak, the quality of which varied according to his social standing. The ordinary cloak was perfectly plain whereas among the upper classes it would have elaborate patterns, with fancy edges and trimmings.

One authority on the Aztecs believes that the wearing of clothes was so regulated that it would have been possible, by looking at a person's dress and ornaments, or the lack of them, to tell exactly who the wearer was, what trade or profession he followed, where he came from, and a good deal about his character and wealth. This is not so strange since, a century or more ago, the same informed guess could often have been made about an individual from the United States or Europe, just by glancing at the cut and style of the clothes the person was wearing.

Nowadays, this would not be so easy. Nevertheless, provided both were in full dress uniform, no one could mistake an army private for a general. So it was with people in the Aztec Empire: one glance was usually enough. Among the unmistakable signs were the many ornaments and decorations — not to mention the gold plugs for ear, nose, and lip — habitually worn by the upper classes.

FACE AND HAIR STYLES

High-ranking soldiers often made up their faces with black, red, or yellow paint; or they might print patterns on their cheeks with a clay stamp smeared with color. Girls sometimes used yellow face paint as well, and even spread red paint on their teeth. But unless it was a wedding-day decoration, this habit was frowned upon by their elders.

An Aztec nobleman (left), a farmer (right), and a woman (foreground).

Ordinary people of both sexes wore their hair short at the front and long at the back. Married women plaited their hair and pinned it in place at the sides of the head.

Small boys up to the age of about eight had their dark hair trimmed in an upside down bowl-like haircut. When they were older, they wore distinctive tresses; and the mature warrior allowed these to dangle collar length at the back. The front was trimmed to about mid-forehead length and the rest of the hair gathered into a topknot, bound by a headband. Since most Native Americans do not have very much facial hair, shaving was not necessary, and the odd hairs were simply plucked out.

FEATHERS

The nobles also made great use of birds' feathers for personal adornment. Green and red feathers from the tropics were very high on the list of tribute to be paid by a defeated tribe. Commoner feathers were often dyed. In addition to being used for trimming blouses, capes, and headdresses, the feathers were glued or sewn onto material, so that an entire garment might appear to be made of plumage. Unfortunately, feathers do not survive naturally for long periods of time, nor did they escape the zealous heathen-hunting Spanish missionaries immediately after the conquest.

Some feathered objects, however, have come down to us. Shields were often elaborately feathered into designs and pictures. One that has survived shows an animal in blue feathers on a red feather background. Each part has been carefully outlined with narrow ribbons of gold. Cortés, the conqueror of the Aztecs, was given it, among other things, by Moctezuma and sent it to the Emperor Charles V in Europe. It can be seen today in an Austrian museum.

Warriors sometimes carried feathered fans and are shown going into battle bearing an enormous wickerwork structure on their shoulders. It was commonly decked with ornaments and plumage and rose a couple of feet above the head. This arrangement cannot have allowed the warrior great freedom of movement.

CHAPTER 8

Growing Up

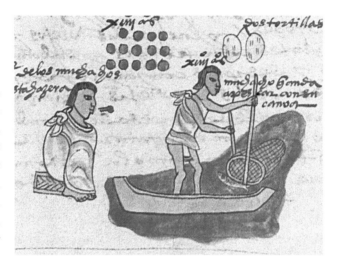

A father teaching his son to fish from a canoe.

All Aztec children, whether rich or poor, and both boys and girls, began life in much the same way. They were helped into the world by a midwife and named on a lucky day picked out by an astrologer or fortune-teller.

The Aztecs were aware that there were 365 days in a solar year. They calculated on the basis of eighteen months, each of twenty days, which come to 360 days. Therefore, they had to add another five days, which they called *nemontemi*. These days were considered to be extremely unlucky. So people preferred to stay at home. No important projects were started at those times.

DATES AND NAMES

The *tonalpohualli*, or religious year, which was made up of 260 days, also contained a number of unlucky days. For example, if a male child was born on rabbit day 2, he would die young as a drunkard. If his birthday was on jaguar day 1, he would grow up to be captured in battle and killed. No naming took place on these and other inauspicious days. To balance this, however, there were also days that were regarded as especially lucky.

The new baby was named after the day when the ceremony was held, for instance, flint knife 4, alligator 2, and so on. But because a large number of babies were born and named on the same day, something had to be done to tell them apart. It was ridiculous telling a stranger that your name was deer 3, since a great many other children were also called deer 3. For this reason, an extra, individual, and personal name was given as well as the official date name.

PREPARATION FOR LIFE

Girl babies, as it has been shown, were given birth presents of miniature sewing, darning, and cleaning equipment. Boy babies, too, were given gifts pointing to their likely roles in life. These varied according to the class and profession of the father. A boy was almost always fated to follow in his father's footsteps and to do the same job as he did. A potter's son, therefore, would be presented with toy clay pots, and a basket maker's son with tiny versions of the containers made by his father. A warrior's male heir was officially received into that class with the gift of a small spear, spear-thrower, shield, and some arrows.

In ordinary households, boys were expected to help their sisters around the home with simple tasks such as collecting firewood and sweeping the floor. At about the age of eight, they would go to a school known as the *telpochcalli* where, in addition to some military training, they were taught practical subjects such as basic

Young boys of eight and upward were taught practical crafts and given military training at the telpochcalli.

farming (with weeding of the school gardens as a priority) and various crafts like pottery, carpentry, weapon making, and building.

No boy could marry until he had mastered his craft and thus served a kind of apprenticeship, probably at the age of twenty or thereabouts. He would have to satisfy the local authorities that he was a qualified builder, silversmith, or whatever. They would then grant him permission to marry and loan him a piece of land sufficient to support himself and his future wife and children.

THE CALMÉCAC

Male children of upper-class families also started school at the age of eight. The discipline of the *calmécac*, as it was called, was very strict. Pupils ate corn pancakes (the modern Mexican tortillas) and drank nothing but water. At about this time, boys from noble families also had their earlobes, noses, and lower lips pierced for the wearing of gold plugs of various designs.

In pictures of children that survived the Spanish invasion, their ages are shown by putting one little blue circle (usually above the drawing of the head) for each year. Another method of denoting age was to add a sketch of the number of tortillas per day that a child was permitted to eat. The scale was as follows:

Age in years	0-3	3-5	5-13	13+
Number of tortillas	$1/2$	1	$1^1/_2$	2

Pupils at the calmécac had to sleep on the hard floor and were often made to go without food for two or three days at a time. The pupils were also awakened during the night to pray.

To encourage self-discipline, the teacher-priests urged the youngsters to drive sharp-pointed cactus thorns into their earlobes and tongues until they drew blood. The spots of blood were often flicked into a sacred fire.

The boys were taught Aztec history, religious hymns, and prayers. Those who intended, when grown-up, to become priests themselves were expected to sacrifice small animals to the gods in practice for the time when they would have to dispatch their fellow human beings.

They learned the order of the days and

months by committing to memory a sort of jingle — rather like our "Thirty days hath September, April, June, and November..." but a little more complicated. They studied the heavens, too, so as to be able to keep track of the seasons, to become familiar with lucky and unlucky stars and planets, and to predict eclipses. Adult priests were not only responsible for informing people about the correct time to sow seed, and to harvest crops but were also supposed to warn them of coming droughts, hurricanes, and any other disasters likely to occur.

Boys attending the calmécac were fortunate in the number of professions open to them. They could, for example, become priests, architects, masons, engineers, scribes, civil servants, sculptors, musicians, or artists.

At the age of fifteen, though sometimes much earlier if they intended to become outstanding warriors or part of the small standing army, all boys were given some military training. They practiced with harmless versions of adult weapons — plain wooden clubs, swords, and small round shields. Later they would go on to use the heavy wooden club studded with sharp blades. Similarly, they had to learn accuracy with

ABOVE: Aztec boys helping out in the practical task of digging a canal.
LEFT: Young people learning to store corn in case of famine.

the spear by throwing at a target over and over again. Military school discipline was as harsh as that in the calmécac. Boys had to obey orders without question, learning to be humble and obedient by performing lowly and unglamorous tasks. They might help out with cleaning temples, public buildings, or causeways, digging canals, strengthening embankments, or clearing ditches. They were also expected to assist their parents in and around the house, perhaps giving a hand on the farm or doing odd jobs in the course of a father's business. But whereas most boys would adopt a profession, those

who became permanent warriors were expected to do little as grown-ups apart from fighting in the frequent wars.

PARENTAL ADVICE

Aztec parents were always exhorting their children to behave well. This is known from one set of rules that has come down to us illustrating the sort of advice they received:

Respect your parents at all times.

Don't set a bad example to your younger brothers and sisters.

If someone tells you a secret, don't tell it to another person.

Don't interrupt when another is speaking, particularly if he or she is of an older generation than your own. However, don't do so even if the speaker is the same age as yourself. In both cases, wait for a pause in the conversation before joining in.

Look after those who are not as fortunate as yourself — for instance, the poor and the sick.

Don't make fun of someone with a disability. Don't mock the deaf or the stutterers; the same thing may happen to you one day.

If someone asks you a direct question, answer directly and honestly.

Don't pull faces or make impolite gestures.

Work well and diligently.

Walk proudly and peacefully.

This is still considered good advice for young people today.

CHAPTER 9

Town and Country

People convicted of certain crimes were sometimes sold, with yokes around their necks, as slaves in the market.

All ranks of Aztec society, from royalty and nobility down, depended for their food and other necessities of life — houses, furniture, clothing, pottery, weapons, jewelry, and much else — on the laboring classes of town and country. Farmers and craftsmen worked hard and for long hours to provide Tenochtitlán and the other main cities with basic goods and comforts. Nobles and wealthy merchants obviously enjoyed a much higher standard of living than farmers and laborers. And there must have been many instances of extreme poverty. Yet, judging from what we are told, it may be fair to conclude that many Aztec farmers lived and worked in better conditions than European peasants of the same period. They certainly had access to a more varied and, presumably, healthier diet.

THE DAWN CHORUS

Town and country dwellers alike probably rose at dawn, awakened by the sunlight shining into the house or hut. In a city such as Tenochtitlán, the wealthier nobles lived in the houses nearest to the marketplace, the temple square, the royal palace, and the public buildings. Farther out were those nobles of more modest means. The city craftsmen were housed in the outer ring of suburbs. And outside the city proper, across the causeways and out in the country were the many "floating islands," made from the lake-bottom mud, on which the farmers built their huts.

The Aztecs had no way of telling the time other than by observing the position of the sun and stars. Midday was easily determined by the height of the sun in the sky, but it was not so simple to calculate when midnight had arrived. In the cities, the authorities therefore ordered a system of signals to be sounded by men beating drums and playing shrill notes on instruments similar to recorders or low notes on conch shells collected from the seashore. The music would blare out at regular intervals — at dawn, mid-morning, noon, sunset, the onset of darkness, midnight, and just before dawn. The reason for the pre-dawn signal was that many daily activities, including trials in the king's courts, began as the sun came up, and people needed time to awaken and get ready.

COURTS OF LAW

Anyone could attend a court hearing but, in practice, few workmen could spare the time to do so. Cases were heard by a judge who was paid from the income of farmland especially set

Craftsmen and laborers building a farmer's hut. Note the elaborate and distinctive roof.

aside for the purpose. This was to ensure that the judge gave his verdict fairly after listening to all the evidence. However, if the judge was found to have acted unfairly, he would be punished severely. So was anyone found guilty of having given false evidence. In addition, to make sure that no one was poisoned by persons trying to affect the outcome of the trial, the king's own kitchens prepared the meals for all those taking part.

The code of laws in Tenochtitlán was adapted from similar codes already being used in neighboring cities such as Texcoco. Serious crimes such as murder, violence, or treason were punished with the death sentence, lesser offenses by fines. Another sentence was slavery. The guilty person was put up for sale in the market with a wooden yoke around his neck. Once sold, if he got the chance, he might make a bid to escape, and only the man who had bought him was allowed to give chase. Should he manage to reach the royal palace, he was set free. If a slave had to be sold three times because of continued misconduct, he was likely to be sacrificed.

Crimes such as theft were not the only reason for being made a slave. A man might suffer this humiliation simply because he was a lazy worker. People sometimes sold themselves for food and shelter. Merchants occasionally bought slaves when they were on trading journeys. Most men taken in battle were sacrificed to the gods but sometimes became slaves.

MERCHANTS

Although nobles regularly bought slaves to work on their farms, merchants were looked down upon because they made a business of buying and selling slaves along with their other goods. Some merchants became rich as a result of profitable trading expeditions and were even permitted to send their sons to the calmécac.

Merchants seem to have been unpopular. There was a legend among the Aztecs that merchants dared not let others know how well off they were. A few occupied grand houses, but most disguised their true condition by wearing the cheapest of clothes and living in simple surroundings. Some were said to unload the proceeds of a business trip during the hours of darkness and often at the house of a friend.

FARMERS

Only the nobles owned land personally, and they worked it with slaves or paid farmhands. The average farmer might have land to farm, but it was only on loan to him. When he died, it went back to the local council of elders to be shared out again to the next generation of farmers.

Farmers' huts were made of wood with a thatched roof. There was only one room, with no chairs (furniture was for nobles), perhaps some boxes in which to keep small private possessions, and household objects such as loom weights, pots, pans, baskets, a grindstone, and a griddle. The family slept and sat on woven rush mats on the hard dirt floor, and there was a central fire around which they all ate. Digging sticks for farm-work and possibly hunting gear or fishing nets would be hung on the wall. There would probably be a recess in the wall for the figure of the family's own local god.

The doorway opening was covered by a blanket, and huts were normally built in groups with

A farmer using a digging stick.

their entrances facing onto a small courtyard or patio. Some families might be able to afford a sauna in their tiny yard. This would have to be constructed, not of wood, but of adobe, or mud bricks, because a fire had to be lit against the back wall. When the wall was hot, water was dashed over it to create steam inside the sauna. The bather then sweated out the dirt, aiding the process by whipping his or her body with thin branches. This kind of treatment was often prescribed to cure a variety of illnesses.

Work began at dawn, and two or three hours' morning work would be broken by a meal of *atolli*, or corn cereal. The main evening meal was cooked on a hot stone or clay griddle. It consisted basically of corn flour tortillas, sometimes dipped into a dish of hot peppers and tomatoes, with plenty of chilies and beans. There were no domestic animals, but the occasional fish, duck, home-raised turkey, or rabbit might be served.

Huts stood on small artificial "floating" islands around a main natural island. Since the farmland close to the home was surrounded by water, a dugout canoe was probably a necessity. A farmer would use his canoe to go duck hunting or fishing. A farming family bringing produce into Tenochtitlán or wishing to attend a religious service or watch a multiple sacrifice would either walk across the wide causeways or paddle almost all the way into the city center.

Chapter 10

The Creation Myth

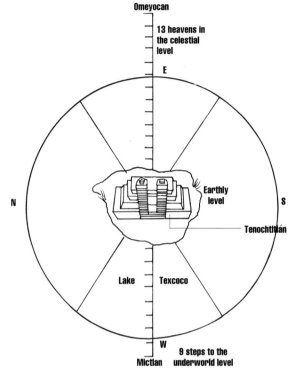

Representation of the Aztec worldview, showing Tenochtitlán at the center.

Most people in the Christian world, up to a few centuries ago, believed firmly in the literal truth of the stories the Bible told about the creation of the world including the first plants, animals, and humans. Many still do. People of other civilizations, all over the world and at different periods of history, believe in their own versions of the creation of the universe. Legends of superhuman beings, gods, and goddesses, and spirits of nature have been passed down from generation to generation. In Mexico, the Aztecs, too, had their own legends about how the world had begun and how the gods had brought the Aztec nation into existence.

THE AZTEC UNIVERSE

The Aztecs believed in twenty-three levels of existence, made up of thirteen heavens, one world, and nine underworlds. The world in which they lived was divided into a number of areas. There were three main divisions up and down from the center of Tenochtitlán, which they held to be the hub of the universe. The vital center around which all else revolved was the holy pyramid temple. It was situated in the exact middle of the capital city and therefore also of the entire Aztec world.

The real world that lay at ground level comprised Tenochtitlán itself, the Aztec lands that surrounded the lake, and the volcanoes in the mountain ranges around the valley. Apart from these three main divisions, visible to all, there were four imaginary quarters, also centered on the great pyramid temple. Each quarter represented a compass direction — east was where the sun rose and west where it set; to the south lay the hot lands and to the north the cold lands. Each quarter possessed its own god and its special sign. The eastern area was ruled by the red Tezcatlipoca, whose symbol was a reed, the western area by the white Tezcatlipoca, or Ehecatl-Quetzalcóatl, god of the wind, whose sign was a house. The north was governed by the black Tezcatlipoca, distinguished by a flint knife, the south by the blue Tezcatlipoca, whose badge was a rabbit.

THIRTEEN HEAVENS

Above this real and recognizable world was an invisible realm — the dwelling place of the gods — divided into thirteen different levels. In the first heaven was to be found the moon and the clouds; in the second the stars. The sun was in the third heaven and the planet Venus in the fourth. Above that was the home of the comets and shooting stars. The sixth and seventh heavens were distinguished only by colors — either a combination of blue and black or blue and green. The eighth heaven was believed to be the place where tempests and tropical hurricanes had their origins. The uppermost heavenly layers, numbers nine to thirteen, were known as *Omeyocan* and were the actual homes of the gods.

The land of the dead was named *Mictlan*, and its lord was Mictlantecutli. This underworld contained nine separate levels, the lowest of which were reserved for common people who were not lucky enough to have been sacrificed or to have been killed in battle. A woman could only escape this fate if she died while giving birth to a child. Aztec religious leaders believed that the entire universe was created, owned, and controlled by the gods.

THE AZTEC GODS

The number of deities recognized and worshiped by the Aztecs varies according to different accounts. One version indicates that apart from the most important deities, notably Huitzilopochtli, Tezcatlipoca, and Quetzalcóatl, there were four divine persons responsible for creation and fifteen fertility gods. These included Coatlicue, mother of Huitzilopochtli, six rain gods — essential for the growing of crops —

The two shrines at the top of the Great Temple.
In the shrine of the god Huitzilopochtli (right) a human sacrifice is being performed, with the victim's blood pouring down the steps.

three fire gods, and four in charge of the drink, pulque. Then there were twelve deities of planets and stars, six gods and goddesses of death, and about a dozen others. Different accounts list more than 120 divine beings, not counting the numbers of strictly regional or family gods. In addition to their normal functions, many of the deities were also given responsibility for the hours of the day and night, and for individual days and weeks of the sacred Aztec calendar.

THE STORIES OF CREATION

The early history of the Aztecs, like that of other societies who lived in the area both before and afterward, is a blend of fact, religion, and myth. And just as there are conflicting accounts of their origins and travels, so there are many versions of the creation of the Aztec universe, of how the gods came into existence, and in turn created human beings.

According to one well-known story, there were four ages or "suns" before the present one, each of them named from the disaster that brought it to an end. The earliest deities were self-created, although the legend does not say how. They dwelt in the universe of the first sun, known as the jaguar sun, after the animals that destroyed it by eating up the giants who also lived there.

The second age was the wind sun. It ended when the lowly nut-eating people of that time were turned into monkeys and blown away by fierce hurricanes.

Fire sun was the name of the third phase of creation. This universe was ruled by Tláloc. His subjects are supposed to have been dogs, birds, and butterflies that lived on lake weeds. Tláloc's world, in turn, was burned by showers of fire from above. This may have been a memory of some disastrous volcanic eruption.

The fourth was the water sun, when the universe was inhabited by more nut- and seed-eaters. The water sun deity was a water goddess, and her world was destroyed by a great flood that covered the entire earth, causing all the people to turn into sea creatures of various kinds.

The present world or sun, so the Aztecs believed, was brought into being by the gods

Quetzalcóatl, the Feathered Serpent, and Tez-catlipoca, the Great God. They were at war with the other gods, and they decided to recreate the world in order to give them an advantage over their enemies.

Another tale describes how these two deities dried up the floodwaters from the previous sun and pushed up the sky. One version says they did this by turning themselves into enormous trees, another says into immensely long and powerful snakes. In this second form, the gods dived into the waters, which had now become the sea, and fought with the earth monster, a gigantic toadlike creature called Cipactli. They split the monster in two and formed the sky and earth from the parts. The other gods were out-raged and ordered that Cipactli should provide all that human beings needed. Grass and flow-ers grew from her skin and trees from her hair. Her eyes spurted streams and springs, and from her mouth flowed great rushing rivers. Her back and shoulder blades made the volcanoes and mountains. The monster complained that no corn should grow and no tree bear fruit until

ABOVE: A turquoise mask of Quetzalcóatl the beneficent, sun god, and one of the creators of the Aztec universe.
LEFT: Tláloc, god of water and vegetation, the most ancient of the Aztec deities.

she had been fed with hearts torn from the human beings who had not yet appeared. The creator gods agreed, and Tezcatlipoca used his bow and drill to make fire, thus bringing light to the dark new world.

THE BLOOD SACRIFICE

One widely believed legend about the final cre-ation of humankind told how Quetzalcóatl went down to the underworld to collect the burned remains of the previous sun's people. The bones were ground into powder and mixed with the ashes. The resulting dust was collected in a huge pot, and the gods stabbed themselves with stone daggers. Their blood dripped into the jar, and after a few days a living boy and girl appeared.

An Aztec god on a raft being pulled by sea serpents.

In another story, the gods produced the race of Aztecs by throwing themselves into a great furnace. The new human beings formed from the fire were expected to show their gratitude by presenting the gods with a gift of equal value. Unless the gods were fed more and more hearts from sacrifice victims, they would destroy the universe all over again. The Aztecs feared such a happening and thus believed that continual sacrifice was absolutely essential to their very existence.

According to yet another tale, Huitzilopochtli, who made the sun rise at dawn and set at dusk after its journey across the sky, had to fight for his life at the start of each day, only to die every evening at sunset. If the god was willing to shed his blood for his people, argued the priests, then it was their duty to shed blood from human hearts for their savior.

A final legend told of the departure of the god Quetzalcóatl, who was driven out of heaven and who sailed away to the east on a raft drawn by serpents. His last words were a vow that he would one day return to reclaim his own. This "one day" would come at the end of the last "century" of the fifth sun. It was an event eagerly awaited by the people. The god's prophecy was to play an important part in the final destruction of the Aztec Empire.

CHAPTER 11

Crafts and Trades

A sacrificial knife with a blade made from obsidian.

When a tribe depends merely on hunting animals and gathering fruit, nuts, roots, and seeds, it can easily be self-sufficient. But when it learns to grow crops and develops into a complex society, there comes a time when ordinary people can no longer provide themselves with all the things they need.

To take an example: a man might envy the chipped-stone spearheads that his friend makes. Other hunters also admire the workmanship, and soon the "expert" is making spearheads for the whole tribe. He is rewarded by extra shares of meat when a kill is made. Or it might be that someone is better than others at weaving baskets and begins to produce them for friends, who in their turn do the basket weaver's share of hunting, fishing, and gathering.

As the years pass, the expert craftsmen spend all their working hours at their own particular skills. This is almost certainly how the Aztecs developed their crafts. As we have seen, a boy usually took on his father's job and was trained in that craft at the telpochcalli. As soon as he proved himself competent to earn a living and support a family, he was permitted to marry.

The craftsman would display his goods in the market, which was visited by thousands of people in a single day. If the goods were of decent quality, the craftsman could expect to sell or exchange them for things that were equally valuable.

CANOES

A dugout canoe was an essential possession, both for personal transportation and also for carry-

ing foodstuffs and craft work to and from the market. It is not known exactly how an Aztec craftsman made a canoe, but it was quite likely that he had to start by felling a suitable tree and chopping off a length of trunk. This cannot have been easy, because it had to be done with an ax made either of the softish metal, copper, or of obsidian, a razor-sharp but rather brittle stone.

The trunk was split in half lengthwise with chisels or wedges and the inside of each section hollowed out. A favorite method of doing this was to drop red-hot stones onto the wood. When sufficiently blackened and charred, the

An Aztec farmer's house.

45

wood was scraped away with a chisel or stone.

Canoes varied in length, beam, and carrying capacity, according to the use to which they were put. Small canoes were used for single paddlers, medium-sized ones for whole families, and large, barge-like ones for transporting heavy loads of farm produce, pottery, and building materials.

BUILDERS AND STONEMASONS

There must have been a good demand for specialists in building materials. Ordinary people lived in simple wooden huts with thatched roofs. Still someone had to chop and trim the posts and boards, and to collect and put the bundles of reeds in place. Craftsmen had houses made of adobe, or sun-dried brick. Only the nobles owned stone hous-

ABOVE: This stone statue of the god Huehueteotl shows the detail Aztec sculptors could achieve. BELOW: Farmers used canoes to bring produce to market.

es, and they would have employed men skilled in carving the stone from the mountains around Tenochtitlán.

Those who shaped stones were of different grades of ability. There were plenty of ordinary laborers who knocked the boulders into straight-edged blocks with copper tools or fist-shaped lumps of harder stone. The finer work was done for palaces and public buildings. There were also statues and images of the gods to be carved. Detail was achieved by wearing away the stone with wet sand on a strip of strong but flexible leather. Other stone workers chipped and shaped obsidian, chalcedony, and similar stones into the knife blades used by the priests to perform human sacrifices, or into long, sharp slivers for setting in war clubs.

ABOVE: A metalworker casting an ax by using a blowpipe to increase the fire's temperature so that the molten copper pours into a mold.
RIGHT: Feather workers. Feathers were used to adorn many types of clothing, both for nobles and commoners.

SMITHS

There must also have been copper smelters, for the only metal tools used by the Aztecs were made of this comparatively soft metal. Gold and silver were also worked by smiths, but the Aztecs did not attach the same high value to these metals as the Europeans did, and still do. Aztec lords preferred to wear green quetzal feathers to gold, although they did wear gold and silver body and face ornaments as well. So goldsmiths and silversmiths concentrated on making decorations for the king and his nobles.

It is interesting to note that in Tenochtitlán, as in most historic cities elsewhere, the various craftsmen — carpenters, smiths, potters — tended to live close to others in the same trade. It was

The mask of the god Xipetotec, patron of goldsmiths.

convenient for someone in search of a silver ornament to go straight to the silversmiths' quarter. It was handy, too, from the workers' point of view, since they could help one another in case of trouble and hope to attract more customers who were perhaps just looking.

Among other tradesmen in Tenochtitlán were foresters, wood-carvers and furniture makers, potters, tailors, and sandal makers. In addition there were feather and obsidian mirror workers, mat weavers and papermakers, charcoal burners, scribes, insignia makers, and jewelers.

47

CHAPTER 12

Cortés and the Conquest

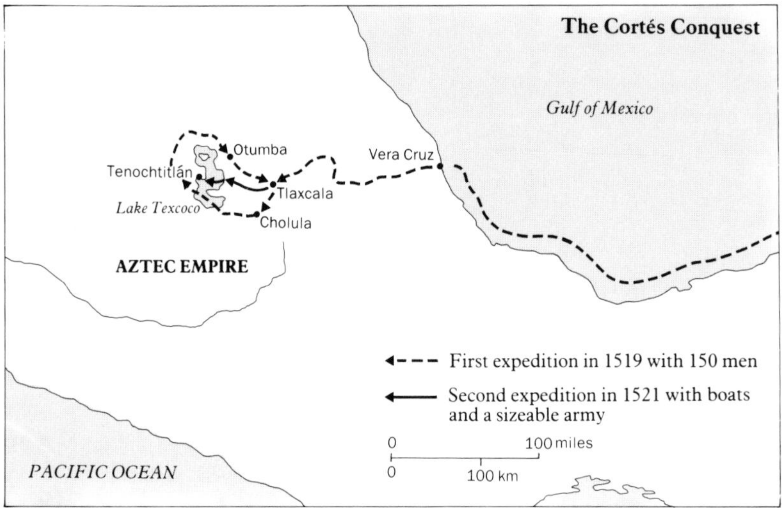
The Cortés Conquest
Gulf of Mexico
Otumba
Vera Cruz
Tenochtitlán
Tlaxcala
Lake Texcoco
Cholula
AZTEC EMPIRE
First expedition in 1519 with 150 men
Second expedition in 1521 with boats and a sizeable army
0
100 miles
0
100 km
PACIFIC OCEAN

Map of the Cortés conquest.

In the late fifteenth century, Christopher Columbus, an Italian by birth, thought he could reach the continent of Asia by sailing westward from Europe instead of eastward, around Africa, the normal route so far followed by European seamen, notably those from Portugal. Columbus knew the world was round, but he had great difficulty in convincing various European heads of state that the idea was sound enough for them to finance an experimental voyage. Eventually, King Ferdinand and Queen Isabella of Spain proved sympathetic and provided three ships for the trip.

In the course of four voyages between 1492 and 1502, Columbus reached the islands of the Caribbean and claimed them for Spain. In due course, Spaniards established settlements on the larger islands, notably Colba (Cuba) and Hispaniola (Haiti and the Dominican Republic). On his last voyage, Columbus sailed along the east coast of Central America. Spain and its rival naval power, Portugal, both claimed the right to explore and settle the lands across the Atlantic. After Columbus died, Spaniards flocked across the ocean, using the Caribbean islands as bases from which to colonize the New World, to convert Native Americans to Christianity, and to make fortunes for themselves.

SIGNS AND PROPHECIES

In 1518 Spaniards sailed from Cuba on a raiding voyage to the coast of Mexico. It was to have a dramatic and disastrous effect on the lives of the Aztecs.

Although Tenochtitlán was miles inland, news of the arrival of strangers quickly reached the ears of the Aztec authorities. Messengers from the coast brought reports to the capital of mountains or great castles moving through the sea. It is obvious to us today that these mysterious objects were really the galleons of the Spaniards. Moctezuma called the messengers liars and had them executed.

The king, nevertheless, was uneasy. A bright new comet was sighted in the sky. He asked his fortune-tellers what it meant. They could give no satisfactory answers, so Moctezuma had them thrown into wooden cages and left them to die of hunger.

Then there was a strange storm on the lake. Huge waves crashed against the shore although there was no wind. Many people died. Even harder to explain was the reported capture of a bird with a stone mirror as its head. The mirror reflected stars, even in bright sunlight. The king of Texcoco, the neighboring town, said that all these signs were warnings of approaching disaster.

Another disturbing message was that the new-

Spanish galleons (or "mountains in the sea") of the type that brought Cortés and his soldiers to the coast of Mexico.

comers were half men and half deer. This was clearly a reference to the horses of the Spaniards. The Aztecs' reaction was probably the same as that of the ancient inhabitants of Greece the first time they saw horses being ridden. The sight then had given birth to the fanciful idea of a race of centaurs. Horses had once roamed wild throughout the Americas but had been extinct for thousands of years. The Aztecs, of course, had never heard of centaurs or horses.

Then came other rumors describing the appearance on the coast of a man who resembled the god Quetzalcóatl, together with his retainers. Moctezuma was concerned that the ancient prophecy of Quetzalcóatl, that he would return "one day," was about to come true. This momentous event could bring about a great upheaval and possibly a change of power. When the king's messengers returned from collecting taxes and tribute in the Vera Cruz area, they assured their royal master that Quetzalcóatl had indeed returned.

"Quetzalcóatl," it turned out, was the Spanish adventurer Hernán Cortés, who, in 1519, had sailed with his followers from Cuba and landed at a place that he named Vera Cruz. This means "True Cross," and it suggests that while the Spaniards were looking for treasure, they were also coming as missionaries.

GIFTS AND GUNS

By now, Moctezuma, who was convinced that Cortés was the returning god, sent emissaries from Tenochtitlán who offered Cortés the cloth-

ing and ornaments that Quetzalcóatl was supposed to have worn. When the Spaniards asked
pointedly whether the feathers and other finery
were all they were to receive, the ambassadors
replied that this was all there was. Cortés invit-
ed them on board his ship and ordered his largest
cannon to be fired. The terrified envoys were
then challenged to fight duels with the Spanish
soldiers with steel swords. They politely declined
and scrambled over the side of the ship and down
into their canoes. As fast as they could, they made
their way back to Tenochtitlán.

Moctezuma was no longer convinced that the
leader of the invaders was really Quetzalcóatl.
He ordered his sorcerers to make magic spells
that would either kill Cortés or, at least, drive
him away. These were unsuccessful. Cortés
demanded more gifts and actually sent the king
a Spanish helmet, suggesting it be filled with
gold dust.

The king's attitude kept changing — one
minute he seemed prepared to worship the
strangers and load them down with gold, the
next he was plotting to kill them. The gifts of
gold merely strengthened Cortés's resolve to
reach the Aztec capital.

THE MARCH TO TENOCHTITLÁN

The Spaniards possessed many advantages. They
had the great guns that had so scared the Aztec
envoys. They had soldiers, protected by armor,
who fought with assorted weapons including
handguns, steel swords, and crossbows. The
Spanish cavalry was more mobile than the Aztec
infantry. But perhaps the biggest advantage that
Cortés enjoyed was that some of the tribes of
central Mexico disliked the Aztecs and were willing to help the invaders to defeat them. In no
other way could a band of some 600 adventur-
ers have conquered such a vast empire.

In the early summer of 1519, Cortés led his
men inland. Their first pitched battle was against
the warriors of Tlaxcala. The Tlaxcalans began
by trying to cast spells on the invaders. Then
they followed the advice of their astrologers, who
told them the enemy was powerless at night.
The wizards were wrong on both counts. The
two sides made peace, and Moctezuma was
astonished to learn that the Tlaxcalans, who had
once fought his own troops to a standstill, had
been easily overwhelmed by the foreigners.

After this first encounter, it was clear that a

Armed Spanish invaders of Cortés's army on horseback — the sight that so terrified the Aztecs.

basic difference in tactics gave the Spaniards an additional edge over their opponents. While the Aztecs tried desperately to capture prisoners for sacrifice, the Europeans aimed only to kill their enemies as quickly as possible. On one occasion, Cortés was actually captured. He could easily have been killed and the invasion smashed. Instead, he was rescued by his own men as the Aztecs were about to hustle him away.

Cortés and his men eventually reached Tenochtitlán. From this point we know a great deal more about the Aztecs, for the Spaniards kept records and wrote down what they said and did. Moctezuma, still unsure about how to treat them, installed them in his father's old palace. He may have hoped to make them drunk and powerless or even to starve them to death. The Spaniards fired off a couple more rounds from their cannon, which terrified the people.

After a time, things seemed to settle down. Cortés tried, without success, to convert Moctezuma to Christianity. Then news reached the city that some of Cortés's men left behind at Vera Cruz had been slain by Aztec soldiers. Using this as an excuse, Cortés seized the king and chained him up as a prisoner.

Hernán Cortés meets with the nobles of Tlaxcala in 1519.

The Spanish defeat

There was temporary relief for the Aztecs when Cortés left the city to deal with the landing of a Spanish army sent from Cuba to discipline him for his unofficial invasion. Leaving his lieutenant, Pedro de Alvarado, in charge of only eighty soldiers, he marched off to the coast. There he defeated the army from Cuba and added the survivors to his own armed force.

Alvarado, meanwhile, rather stupidly interfered with an Aztec religious ceremony in the capital. Expecting a demonstration near the temple, he arrested the priests and a drummer and cut off their hands. The angry citizens threatened to riot, and Cortés arrived back just in time to stop worse trouble. Moctezuma, now in a more defiant mood, tried to assert his authority again. But when he agreed to go onto the palace roof to appeal for calm, the crowd below, furious at the way their king had given in to the Europeans, started to hurl spears and stones at him. One stone caught him on the arm; another hit his leg; and a third missile smashed his skull and killed him.

Cortés weighed the situation and decided to get his men out as soon as possible. The Spaniards made sure to take all the gold they had received, as well as extra treasures from the

ABOVE: Cortés and his men attack the causeways of Tenochtitlán.
BELOW: Cortés' deputy, Alvarado, takes refuge in the face of a defiant Aztec crowd.

palace. Cortés loaded seven horses with his own share. They left in the middle of the night but were spotted. Aztec guards raised the alarm.

The retreating Spaniards were hampered by their gold. The wooden bridges were not in place across the causeway's gaps. Many slipped into the water and were unable to save themselves because of the weight of the metal. Those in the rear clambered across the piled-up bodies.

Once on the mainland, the Spaniards had the advantage of narrow paths, so that they could only be attacked, a few at a time, from the front or back. Cortés only prevented a total disaster by concentrating his fire on the noble Aztec leaders, figuring that the ordinary soldiers would become dispirited if their leaders were killed. Even so, when the fighting was over, only a quarter of the Spanish force got away. Because the Aztecs stopped to strip the bodies of the fallen, they lost their chance to finish Cortés once and for all. Finally, the survivors straggled back to the friendly territory of Tlaxcala.

THE END OF THE AZTEC EMPIRE

News soon spread of the gold that the defeated Spaniards had carted away. Reinforcements poured into Cortés' camp and by April 1521 a new Spanish army was ready to attack. In Tenochtitlán, the royal council elected Cuauhtémoc, Moctezuma's cousin, to be the next king. Many citizens were confident that the Spaniards would never return. Cortés had other ideas.

This time he attacked all three causeways at once, sending his men, now armed with cannon and muskets, along each one, filling in the gaps with stones. To reduce resistance, he allowed his Native American allies to smash and burn buildings. The Spaniards also had a new weapon. They had transported, piece by piece, the parts of several boats. The vessels were put together on the lake shores and used for the siege of the capital. They blockaded the center, gradually reducing the Aztecs to near-starvation. As the new king tried to make his escape across the lake, he was captured by the Spaniards.

At last, the Spaniards burst through into the city center, met by the stench of decaying bodies left unburied. The survivors were too weak to offer any resistance. By August, Tlatelolco, the last unoccupied Aztec city, had fallen, and the mighty Aztec Empire had come to an end.

CHAPTER 13

Destruction and Conversion

A jaguar knight (right), dressed in the skin of a jaguar, a sacred animal for the Aztecs, was a member of the elite group to whose ranks every brave warrior in the Aztec army aspired.

There are still traces here and there in modern Mexico of the old Aztec culture and religion. For instance, at the feast of San Miguel (St. Michael), a model of a jaguar is paraded around. The jaguar was a sacred animal in Aztec times, and the bravest of the warriors were permitted to join the elite group of jaguar knights. So, although the Spanish authorities did their best to convert the Mexicans to Christianity, echoes of the ancient religion remained. This is usually the case wherever one form of worship is replaced, often forcibly, by another. The hold that earlier religions continue to have on people helps to explain why we still celebrate with holly, ivy, mistletoe, fir trees, and Yule logs at Christmastime.

BUILDING ON THE RUINS

The Catholic authorities who followed in the wake of the invaders decided that in order to introduce their own religion they had to destroy the Aztec temples and the statues of the gods to whom they were dedicated. The victorious Spaniards therefore attacked the pyramid temples and altars of the Aztecs and tore them apart stone from stone. Yet, in many places, as they moved on to the next town, they found that the last temple they had dealt with had been rebuilt during their absence. Although they sometimes erected Christian churches on top of the pyramids, crafty Aztec builders sometimes managed to build a statue of one of their old gods into the wall itself. Even so, the destruction was ruthless and thorough. In 1531 Bishop Juan de Zumárraga boasted that his workmen had demolished more than 500 Aztec temples and reduced to rubble over 2,000 statues of the Aztec gods.

Despite the assault on their places of worship, it proved more difficult to reach the minds of the Aztec people. True, the bloody rites of human sacrifice were brought to an end, but the Aztecs did not immediately respond to the symbols of the Christian faith — crosses, Bibles, and the like. They were told that the Catholic church alone could save them from the devil. Gradually, willingly or otherwise, the people gave way. During the two or three years following the conquest, more than a million Aztecs were baptized. In 1524 a dozen Roman Catholic Franciscans also made headway with conversions. They wore ragged robes and went about

OPPOSITE RIGHT: The Spaniards start to destroy the temples of Tenochtitlán.

barefoot. They were obviously so poor that the downtrodden Aztecs began to feel sympathy for them. The sympathetic feelings worked in both directions.

In the footsteps of the Franciscans came Dominican friars, who went to the trouble of learning Nahuatl, the Aztec language. This was necessary because the Indians were forbidden to learn Spanish. Later missionaries did the same and, as a result, they managed to obtain much valuable information about Aztec life and history that would otherwise have been lost.

The missionaries discovered, for example, that the Aztecs had a great deal of literature, both prose and poetry — something that could not have been guessed merely by looking at their picture writing. In many cases, the friars were able to transcribe the Nahuatl literature into Spanish.

Conversion of the natives continued, but the policy of Charles V's representatives was not consistent. Officially, the Spanish government urged that the Aztecs be treated with kindness. Yet they also insisted that they continue to pay tribute, and harsh methods were often needed. How was a Spanish official expected to be kind and severe at the same time? It must have puzzled the would-be converts as well.

THE DOWNFALL OF CORTÉS

Hernán Cortés had been made captain-general, or governor, of New Spain, as Mexico and some of the southwestern United States was at first called. He decreed that the local people should go on paying the tribute they had formerly brought to Moctezuma, but he reserved it all for himself, giving nothing to his companions, who had helped him in the conquest. He also

forced many of his Aztec subjects to work on his farms without pay.

When Cortés went on an expedition to Honduras, he took with him the captured king, Cuauhtémoc. Rumors reached him of a plot against himself, so he had the last Aztec king of all executed.

The government in Madrid was growing worried by the behavior of Cortés and issued an order that he be banned from Mexico City, as the Spaniards now called Tenochtitlán. New officials were sent from Madrid. As time passed, the fortune hunters were replaced by more honest men. In 1535 Antonio de Mendoza became Spain's first viceroy of the New World. He quarreled with Cortés, who had now returned to Mexico. Cortés died in 1547 and was buried in the land he had won for Spain. Some of his descendants still live there and so do the descendants of Moctezuma. These decendants and many other modern Mexicans still speak the Aztec language, Nahuatl.

A statue of the Virgin of Guadalupe in the Basilica of Guadalupe in Mexico City.

RELIGIOUS COMPROMISE

Many of the missionaries believed strongly that the defeated people should be treated with compassion, not exploited and beaten. They argued, with good reason, that if the Native Americans continued to suffer at the hands of white Christians, they would reject a god who let his worshipers behave so badly. If life was so miserable being a Christian, they might think it better to bring back the old gods. Punishment for any Native American who reverted to the Aztec religion was merciless. The offender could be whipped, thrown into prison, or even executed. It took the humble, barefoot missionaries many years to overcome this problem.

One solution for the Aztecs who appeared to obey the Spanish conquerors yet still believed in Huitzilopochtli and the other Aztec deities was to merge some of the new religious figures with the old. It was easy to offer a prayer to a Christian saint if you said to yourself, "This is not really the holy person of the Christians but our old god in a new disguise." Or you might argue, for your peace of mind, "We've always worshiped many gods: another one is unlikely to make much difference."

Many missionaries found their task easier if they consciously permitted the Aztecs to graft together the two views of the universe. For example, the priests knew that Aztec religious ceremonies involved massive crowds and were held in the open air. So they acted Bible stories in front of huge audiences outside churches.

In 1531 a converted Aztec who had changed his name to Juan Diego was out walking when he had a vision of a beautiful woman in shining white. She spoke to him and told him that she was the Blessed Virgin Mary, Mother of Christ, and that she had come down to earth near Mexico City to reinforce the faith of true believers.

The hill where she had appeared was the holy place of the Aztec goddess, Tonantzín. Since Tonantzín was another name for Coatlicue, the mother of Huitzilopochtli, the Catholic church was at first very suspicious. They were afraid that the uncertain faith of their converts would be tested because they would see the Virgin Mary as a disguised Coatlicue.

The vision of Juan Diego was finally accepted. The Virgin Mary of Guadalupe was received as one of the immortals of the Catholic church and has been venerated there ever since.

Juan Diego's vision of the Virgin of Guadalupe. The Virgin became the symbol of Aztec conversion to Christianity and is still venerated in Mexico today.

THE DESTRUCTION OF TENOCHTITLÁN

In the Aztec capital of Tenochtitlán, the Spaniards relentlessly completed the work begun by Cortés. They smashed temples and shrines, destroyed palaces and great houses, and set fire to much of what was left. They then started to rebuild Tenochtitlán as a Spanish city. A cathedral arose above the remnants of the pyramid temples. Unwilling laborers, who still lived as well as they could in the undestroyed outer suburbs, were employed to drain away the lake.

The name Mexico City was not adopted right away, and the Indians went on calling it Tenochtitlán. In the heyday of the Aztec Empire, it had been one of the world's greatest and most splendid cities. By 1560, a population of around a quarter of a million had shrunk to no more than 75,000. In other words, within the span of two generations, roughly two out of every three people had gone — murdered, starved, dead of disease, or forcibly moved out.

Since the sixteenth century, however, Mexico City has never stopped growing. In 1992 it covered more than 500 square miles and had almost 15 million inhabitants.

CHAPTER 14

Remains of the Aztecs

The Spaniards were so thorough and ruthless in destroying what they considered to be the outward signs of a heathen, devilish creed that today very few pre-conquest Aztec remains are still to be seen.

Some small Aztec objects and statues are now in the National Museum in Mexico City. One interesting discovery was made during excava-

Chichén Itzá, in eastern Mexico, is the site of the remains of temples built by the Mayas centuries earlier but in the same style as those of the Aztecs.

tions at Nonoalco, a district of the capital. The diggers found a large quantity of broken pottery. This is not unusual, for fragments of pots normally come to light where people once lived. The odd thing here was that the pieces made up complete pots and could hardly have been thrown away because of an accident. It appears highly probable, therefore, that the pots were broken on purpose and all at the same time.

The only solution that seemed to fit the facts was worked out when archaeologists dated the

pottery pieces precisely to the year 1507. This coincided with the date of one of the old Aztec fifty-two-year "centuries," the terrible time that threatened world destruction and endless night. Men smashed, burned, or threw away all their possessions, including household pottery.

TEMPLE RUINS

Only a few remains of Aztec buildings have been found. At Chiconauhtla, excavators came across the outlines of the ground-floor plan of a large house, or palace, which contained about thirty rooms. After more than 400 years, it was still possible to see their shapes and sizes.

Most of the Aztec remains scattered through Mexico are those of temples. In spite of Bishop Zumárraga's boast that he had smashed over 500 of them, the fact is that the average temple was too strongly built to be destroyed entirely. Many of the temples were constructed of huge blocks of stone, quarried from the sur-

Recent excavations in Mexico City have revealed the base of the Aztecs' Great Temple.

rounding mountains, and moved into position on rollers. It must have taken the Spaniards more effort and money to destroy the solid stone base of a temple than it did for the Aztecs to put it up in the first place.

It is clear from what remains that the design of an Aztec temple was very similar to that of other Native American societies of Central America. Splendid ruins of temples built by the Mayas, for example, are to be found in Guatemala and at Chichén Itzá in the Mexican state of Yucatán.

The Toltec pyramid at Teotihuacán was apparently dedicated to Quetzalcóatl, the Feathered Serpent, and Tláloc, the rain god, deities later taken over and worshiped by the Aztecs. Around the base are repeated stone carvings of the symbols of both gods.

A calendar, made from stone, excavated on the site of the Great Temple area in Tenochtitlán.

A small Aztec temple survives at Tenayuca, which once stood on the lake's mainland northwest of Tenochtitlán. A shrine to the war god stands on a comparatively small pyramid near Vera Cruz, on the Gulf of Mexico coast.

At Tlatelolco there are large portions of the base of a great pyramid, with parts of even earlier bases. And at Tepoztlán can be seen temple remains which, remarkably, are cut into a hillside.

In the capital itself, digging in 1967 revealed parts of a temple dedicated to Quetzalcóatl. This was carefully incorporated into the design of a subway station and has a cactus garden growing in front of it.

MUSEUM TREASURES

Among the many objects that may be viewed in Mexico's National Museum and abroad in museums of many other countries are a fine stone head of an eagle knight or warrior, a huge calendar stone found in 1790, and also the so-called "national" stone on which it once rested.

Unfortunately, there is very little original Aztec gold work in museums. This is because most of the gold jewelry sent back to Spain from the New World was melted down to pay for the nation's foreign wars in Europe. What little there is comes from the rare tombs of great nobles — for example, those at Oaxaca, about 250 miles southeast of Mexico City.

Rarer still than gold jewelry is the featherwork of which the Aztecs were so proud. Only two genuine pieces have come down to us. One is a shield decorated with the figure of a coyote, made of red and blue feathers with gold fillets around each part. The other example is the famous green quetzal feather headdress given to Cortés by Moctezuma. Both the shield and the headdress were sent to Europe and are now on display at a museum in Vienna, Austria.

The National Museum of Anthropology in Mexico City features an extensive collection of Aztec artifacts including the famous ancient Aztec calendar. This carved stone calendar weighs 20 tons and has a diameter of 12 feet (4 meters). Visitors to London's Museum of Mankind, one of the best collections of Aztec artifacts outside Mexico, will be able to see several stone statues, including a *chacmool*. This is a seated human figure holding a container for receiving sacrificial blood and similar gifts to the gods. But perhaps the most striking of the objects on show here is a human skull patterned with bands of turquoise and lignite mosaic pieces. It may be a representation of the god Tezcatlipoca.

EPILOGUE

In 1978 a team led by Professor Eduardo Matos began to excavate some buildings in the center of Mexico City. The dig was to take four years, and it revealed for the first time something of what was left of pre-conquest Tenochtitlán.

The modern presidential palace is built on top of what was Moctezuma's palace. Today's city streets are some 20 feet (6 meters) above the earliest remains, which can still be reached. This appears to be normal for areas that have long been inhabited. In modern Rome, London, and Jerusalem, for example, some of the ancient Roman road surfaces lie up to 16 feet (5 meters) below the present-day level. What seems to happen is that every time a house or

The chinampas *of Mexico today.*

other building is destroyed, builders start to replace it without clearing away the old rubble. Do that a dozen times over the centuries, and the difference in level is explained.

The diggers in Mexico City wanted to excavate the Great Pyramid. Unfortunately for them, the bottom of the temple is now well below the water level. Although Tenochtitlán's surface water has been drained away, it is still there underground, and it is impossible to dig down very far without reaching it. If engineers had pumped the water away, they might have damaged some of the surrounding buildings. This would have been a pity, since many of them dated back to the earliest years of the Spanish occupation.

Trying to interfere as little as possible with neighboring buildings, the excavators began their work. As they dug, they found statues, statuettes, and various pieces of temple furniture such as the serpent altar and braziers in which human hearts were burned.

The excavators also unearthed some of the staircases and internal stonework, showing clearly that the Aztecs did indeed rebuild their temples by covering up the previous one with a new, larger, and taller structure. In this respect, they behaved just like the ancient Sumerians of the Middle East, who did exactly the same thing with their ziggurat pyramid temples. This resemblance among temples has led some people to say, mistakenly, that the civilizations of Sumer, Egypt, and pre-Columbian America might have been connected with one another. What they do not take into consideration is the fact that people facing the same kinds of problems all over the world probably have tackled them in a similar way.

Another interesting find was an area of paving stones that came to light after being buried for over 400 years. Moreover, at the foot of one of the low walls of the newly unearthed temple was a huge, writhing stone serpent, close to where the altar to Huitzilopochtli once stood. Apart from a great many stone masks and figures, the bottom part of the Aztec tzompantli, or skull rack, was also dug up, complete with its decoration of rows of carved stone skulls.

Visitors to Mexico can see one form of living memorial to the Aztecs. Some of the chinampas or "floating gardens" still survive, and continue to be occupied today by Mexicans who are almost certainly descendants of the farmers who cultivated the islands more than four centuries ago. They even travel about in dugout canoes and keep alive the language of their ancestors.

Glossary

AMATL Paper.

ATLATL A spear-thrower.

ATOLLI Corn cereal, often eaten as a separate meal.

CALMÉCAC School run by priests where Aztec boys of noble birth, aged eight years and upward, were trained for the army, the priesthood, or other professions.

CALPULLI Area in Tenochtitlán occupied by families belonging to a clan. Each calpulli had to provide volunteers for work on public projects.

CHACMOOL A stone statue with a receptacal for burning human hearts.

CHINAMITL An artificial "floating" island made up of a drifting mass of vegetation.

CHINAMPA Spanish word for a "floating" island.

COCHINEAL INSECTS The dead bodies of these insects were used by the Aztecs to make red dye for tinting cloth or fiber.

CONQUISTADOR Spanish word for "conqueror," as applied to the Spanish leaders who conquered parts of America, notably Mexico and Peru, in the sixteenth century.

CUICACALLI A "house of song," or temple school for girls.

HUITZILOPOCHTLI The most important Aztec god.

ICHAN TONATIUH The heavenly paradise which warriors slain in battle or sacrificial victims entered. Also called "The Home of the Sun in the Sky."

MAGUEY A native Mexican cactus, also known as agave, used to make pulque.

MAXTLATL A loincloth worn by Aztec youths and men.

MICTLAN The Aztec land of the dead.

NAHUATL The language of the Aztecs.

NEMONTEMI The "unlucky" end-of-year days.

OMEYOCAN The home of the Aztec gods.

PULQUE An intoxicating drink made from the juice of the maguey cactus.

QUETZALCÓATL Aztec god of learning, priesthood, and the winds.

TAMALE Crushed corn and strongly spiced meat.

TECHCATL Altar stone.

TECPAN The royal palace in Tenochtitlán.

TELPOCHCALLI School where boys of eight years and upward were given military training and taught practical tasks and crafts.

TEQUIUA A seasoned Aztec warrior who had taken four prisoners in battle.

TEZCATLIPOCA The Aztec god called "Lord of the Night" and "Lord of the Smoking Mirror." The young man, selected each year to be the chief victim of sacrificial ritual, impersonated this god.

TONALPOHUALLI The Aztec holy calendar of 260 days.

TORTILLA Corn cake cooked on a griddle, eaten hot and with various fillings.

TZOMPANTLI Skull rack.

Index